SAN ANGELO
A to Z

SAN ANGELO

A to Z

A YOUNG READER'S GUIDE

Linda Thorsen Bond

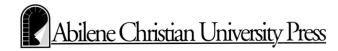
Abilene Christian University Press

SAN ANGELO A TO Z
A Young Reader's Guide

ACU PRESS

ISBN 978-1-68426-011-9
LCCN 2020028877

Printed in the United States of America

LIBRARY OF CONGRESS CATALOGING-IN-PUBLICATION DATA
Names: Bond, Linda Thorsen, author.
Title: San Angelo A to Z : a young reader's guide / Linda Thorsen Bond.
Description: Abilene, Texas : Abilene Christian University Press, [2020]
Identifiers: LCCN 2020028877 | ISBN 9781684260119 (paperback)
Subjects: LCSH: San Angelo (Tex—Juvenile literature. | English
   language—Alphabet—Juvenile literature.
Classification: LCC F394.S15 B66 2020 | DDC 976.4/721—dc23
LC record available at https://lccn.loc.gov/2020028877

Cover and interior design by Sandy Armstrong, Strong Design

For information contact:
Abilene Christian University Press
ACU Box 29138
Abilene, Texas 79699

1-877-816-4455
www.acupressbooks.com

20 21 22 23 24 25 / 7 6 5 4 3 2 1

Acknowledgments

Thank you to these wonderful partners for helping to make *San Angelo A to Z* possible:

Allison Watkins, Tom Green County Extension Agent— Horticulture, Texas A&M AgriLife Extension Service

Berkeley M. Puckett and Sara Beth Terral, Performing Arts Center

Beverly Franklin Allen, M. L. Leddy

Bill Guffey, herd manager, San Angelo State Park

Brian Groves, City of San Angelo

Carl White, Parks and Recreation Director

Concho Valley Photo Club

Courtney Mahaffey, San Angelo Symphony

Del Velasquez and Monica Ramos, Downtown San Angelo, Inc.

Elena Kent, Founding Artistic Director Be Theatre

Howard Taylor and Laura Huckabee, SAMFA

Jim Cisneros, San Angelo State Park Superintendent

Joe Weaver, Fort Concho volunteer

John McEachern, district biologist, Texas Parks and Wildlife

John Osterhous, graphics editing

Kaitlyn Brosh, Howard College

Karl I. Kujawa and Penny Roberts Baker, The Railway Museum

Ken Landon, International Water Lily Collection

Kyle Brock, J. L. Mercer & Sons

Lee Pfluger and Candis Hicks, Heritage Park

Marcy Bosequett, Tom Green County Library System

Maria de los Santos Onofre-Madrid, Spanish translation

Mark Priest, Legend Jewelers

Matt Lewis, President and CEO, San Angelo Area Foundation

Mike and Amy Meyers, Peaceful Valley Donkey Rescue

Rebekah Brackin and Brittney Miller, Angelo State University

Richard and Donna Crisp, Ruffini blueprints

Richard Salmon, Sculpture Garden

Robert Bluthardt and Evelyn Lemons, Fort Concho

Rosendo Ramos, Mariachi Program SAISD

Savannah Logsdon, Marketing Director, Ballet San Angelo

Selina Rojas-McSherry, San Angelo Nature Center

Shannon Strum, West Texas Collection

Stan Meador, Texas Pacifico Transportation

Stone Settle Advertising, Heritage Park graphics

Suzanna Valenzuela, Convention & Visitors Bureau

Tilly Chandler and Gus Clements, Historic Beginnings of San Angelo

Tim L. Vasquez, plane and drone information

Victor Mancilla, Producer, Eravision

Photo Credits

(Front Cover image—**Christine McCormick**; opposite: Pop Art Museum—**Bruce R. Partain**)

Photo Location Key
(the first letter corresponds with the page—A is for Art)
1=left; 2=right
a=above; c=center; b=below

Courtesy of Angelo State University—Chemistry student Eduardo Aguirre Serrata: E1b; Brit Raley holds diploma: E2c; ASU mascots: E2b. **Diann Bayes**—Statue of the Lady in Blue: J1a. **Jim Bean**—Hank the Cowdog and girls reading: H2b. **Linda Thorsen Bond**—Wing mural by Gabriel: W2a. **Shelby Bond**—Current Fort Concho: F1b; Quilters gather at Sierra Vista United Methodist Church: Q1b; Quilter: Q1a. **Susan Brooks**—VW Beetle: A2c; Concho River through downtown: C2c; Troops with huge flag: G2b; Monarchs cluster together: M1b; Ruffini Chapel: O2b; Orient-Santa Fe Depot and train: T2c; Concho River view: X1b; Field of Wild Mustard flowers: Y1b. **Monica Canales**—Alyssa in soccer uniform: U1b. **Airman 1st Class Zachary Chapman**—"Eat-Sleep-Thrive, improving firefighter resilience": G1b. **Courtesy of City of San Angelo**—Firefighters: U2c; Fort Worth Police Pipes & Drums: U2a. **Mike Erb**—Stephens Performing Arts Center: P1b; Etta Joyce Murphey Performance Hall: P2c; Ballet class: P2b. **Fort Concho Archives**—Black and white Fort Concho: F1a; African American "Buffalo Soldiers": F2a; Reenactors in costume: F2c; Early churches designed by Oscar Ruffini: O1b; Texas shepherd in the 1800s: S1b. **Andrea Fryrear**—Cub Scout and Scout Leader: U1b. **Jim Glossbrenner**—Nymphaea Blue Cloud lily: I1b; Librarian at story time: L1a; Girl in wings reading a book: L2a; Carolyn Quillan's flower quilt: Q2c; Quilting machine at Stephens Downtown library: Q2a; Riding a bucking bronco: R2a; Sunrise over the plains: V2c; Cactus in bloom: Y2b. **Courtesy of Historic Beginnings of San Angelo**—Jumano descendants: J1b. **Courtesy of Howard College**—Construction: E1a. **Elena Kent**—Be Theatre's melodrama: P2a. **Glenny Kvalakkat**—Monarch caterpillar: M2b; Monarch chrysalis: M2b; Monarch chrysalis opening: M2b; Monarch coming out of its chrysalis: M2b. **Ken Landon**—Queen Sirikit lily: I2a. **Charles Luker**—Lighted bridge: C1b; Fishing from kayak: C2b; Pond with lilies: I2c; Monarch by yellow flower: M2c; Twin Buttes behind Lake Nasworth: V2b; Bee on Coreopsis flower: Y1a; Wild Yellow Lily: Y2c. **Victor Mancilla, Eravision**—Shooting the film *The Needle and the Thread*: J2a; Marisa Casillas as Maria de Jesus de Ageda from *The Needle and the Thread*: J2b. **Christine McCormick**—Bison mama with her baby: B2c; Crowd on Concho: C1a; Sunset over water: V2a. **John J. Osterhout**—Truck art: A1b; Bison: B1b; Texas Dawn lily: I1c; Olivia McCoy watching model trains: T2a; Police officer Porsche Potts: U1a; Mussel shell from Concho River: X1a; Sculpture of mermaid holding pearl designed by Jayne Beck and sculpted by Garland Weeks: X2a; Inside of shell with pearl: X2b; Pearls and shapes inside shell: X2b; Field of Greenthread flowers: Y2a. **Bruce R. Partain**—Mural Pop Art Museum: A1a; Chicken Farm Art Center: A2a; throwing wheel: A2b; Donkeys in pen: D1a; Mark Meyers with donkey: D1b; Radek Spatz hand-feeds donkeys: D2b; Peaceful Valley Donkey Rescue: D2c; Lakewood HS mariachi band: E2a; Wings of US Air Force: G2c; Information display: H1a; Pocket Park: H2c; Statue of Jumano Chief Tuerto by Vic Payne: J2c; Boy on monkey rings: K1b; Girl in tires: K1a; Children at the park: K2c; Children's area of the library: L1b; Boys looking at exhibits: N1a; Roger the blue and yellow Macaw: N1b; Hydra the Chinese water dragon: N2b; Karma the veiled chameleon: N2c; Roping: R1b; Rodeo parade: R1a; Ambassadors riding horses with Texas flags: R2c; "Welcoming Ewe II" sheep: S2c; "Don't Ewe Mess with Texas" sheep: S2b; RQ-1K Predator drone: W2b; Boots from J. L. Mercer: Z1b; Woman using old-fashioned sewing machine: Z1a; Creating foot print: Z2a; Boot lasts on shelves: Z2c; Creating boots by hand: Z2b. **Mark Priest**—Pearl necklace from Legend Jewelers: X2a. **Airman 1st Class Abbey Rieves**—Science experiment at youth career fair: G2a. San Angelo Standard Times—Oscar Ruffini: O1a. **Stone Settle Advertising**—The Pfluger sons: H1b. **Kenneth Thompson**—Orient-Santa Fe Depot railroad museum: T1b; Windmill and sunset: V1a. **Courtesy of Tom Green County Library**—Stephens Central Branch Library: L2c. **Tim L. Vasquez**—View of San Angelo from above: V1b; T-38 Talon: W1b; Hummingbird: W2c.

Art (El Arte)

A is for Art. In San Angelo, you can look at all kinds of art, watch art being made, and create your own art.

Art in Uncommon Places

decorates the city with unusual art, like mosaics and sculptures. Paintbrush Alley is the site of colorful murals based on the movie *Giant*. The PopArt Museum is an exciting new gallery with murals and sculptures displayed under the open sky.

There aren't any chickens at The Chicken Farm Art Center, but there are a lot of local artists making art creations in the studios of this old chicken farm. Artists paint, sculpt, make pottery, and create works of art with glass, metal, jewels, and wood. Every month, they host a fiesta, and everyone is invited to come meet the artists, eat delicious food, and listen to music.

ART MUSEUM

There is always something exciting happening at the San Angelo Museum of Fine Arts. The building has art inside, outside, and all around. The exhibits at the museum are always changing, so you can see new art all the time. You can also take art classes there.

Bison (El Bisonte)

B is for Bison, the big, wooly animals that have been in San Angelo since the beginning of time.

You can see bison in San Angelo State Park. They roam around the 7,700-acre park eating grass, but they come running when they see the herd boss bringing them bales of hay. Stay behind the fence when they come near you to keep you and the bison safe.

The great grandparents of these American Plains Bison were part of the 30 million bison that lived in Texas over 100 years ago. When settlers moved west, hunters killed so many bison that they nearly disappeared. It's only because of special care that there are 12 adult and 4 baby bison in the San Angelo herd now.

FUN FACT
Bison weigh 1,000–2,000 pounds, are as tall as a car, and can run about 30 miles an hour. That's faster than the fastest track runners in the world!

Buffalo	Bison
Most live in Asia & Africa	Most live in America
No beard	Thick beard
No hump	Large hump
Longer horns	Small short horns
Light fur	Thick fur
Live 25–30 years	Live 13–21 years

Concho River
(El Río Concho)

C is for Concho River, where San Angelo began.

The River Walk is a lovely place with parks and playgrounds. Walkers and joggers can travel along four miles of trails on the riverbanks, and kayakers can paddle through town. On special days like Independence Day, thousands of people gather at the river stage to hear a concert by the San Angelo Symphony. There are also 20 bridges that cross the branches of the Concho. Some bridges are decorated with art and special lighting.

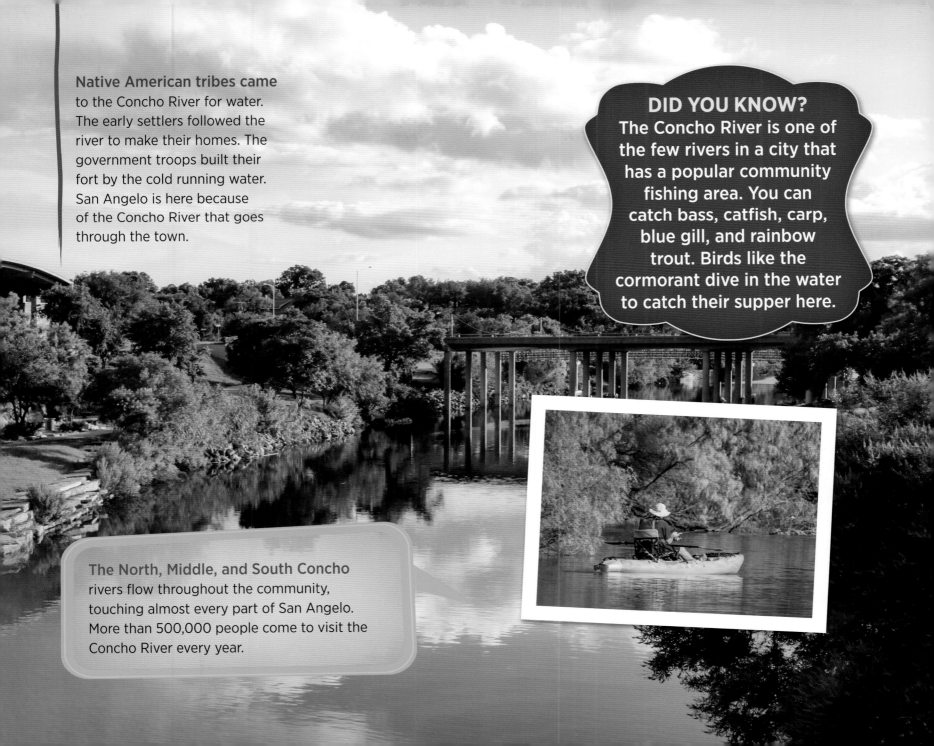

Native American tribes came to the Concho River for water. The early settlers followed the river to make their homes. The government troops built their fort by the cold running water. San Angelo is here because of the Concho River that goes through the town.

DID YOU KNOW?
The Concho River is one of the few rivers in a city that has a popular community fishing area. You can catch bass, catfish, carp, blue gill, and rainbow trout. Birds like the cormorant dive in the water to catch their supper here.

The North, Middle, and South Concho rivers flow throughout the community, touching almost every part of San Angelo. More than 500,000 people come to visit the Concho River every year.

Donkey (El Burro)

D is for Donkey. There are almost 1,000 donkeys at Peaceful Valley Donkey Rescue.

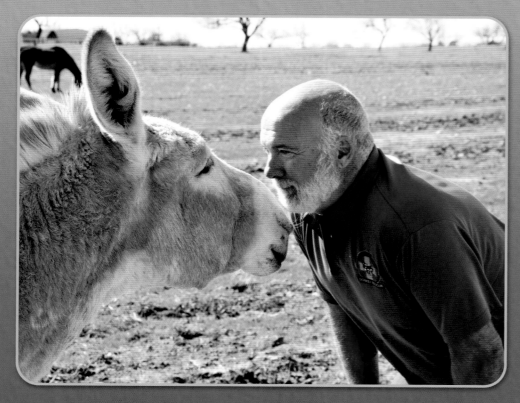

Located just outside San Angelo, Peaceful Valley Donkey Rescue gives abandoned or mistreated donkeys a good life and helps donkeys find new homes. Mark and Amy Meyers have rescued over 13,000 donkeys since 2000 when they opened the rescue, and Mark was named one of CNN's top 10 Heroes for 2019 for his work.

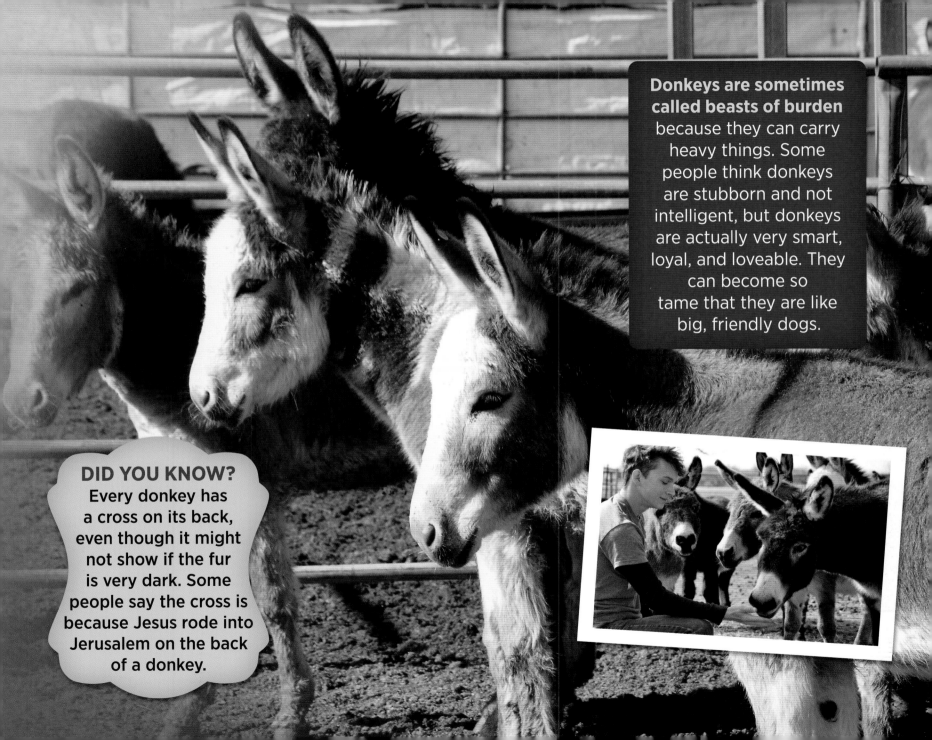

Donkeys are sometimes called beasts of burden because they can carry heavy things. Some people think donkeys are stubborn and not intelligent, but donkeys are actually very smart, loyal, and loveable. They can become so tame that they are like big, friendly dogs.

DID YOU KNOW?
Every donkey has a cross on its back, even though it might not show if the fur is very dark. Some people say the cross is because Jesus rode into Jerusalem on the back of a donkey.

Education (La Educación)

E is for Education, which is very important in San Angelo.

Howard College works hard for its students and the community. Students can learn to be plumbers, electricians, builders, and nurses, and study for many other jobs. There are also classes for people who want to improve in their jobs, change careers, or go to a four-year university.

Angelo State University has 100 different majors, so students can find a subject they love—like math, science, technology, or art—and study with experts in that field. What is your favorite subject to study?

Young Mariachis

The mariachi program is one of the fastest-growing subjects at Lincoln Middle School and Lake View High School, with over 180 students learning to play mari-achi music. Mariachi is rooted in Mexico, but the music attracts students from all backgrounds who want to share their emotions through music and to perform with this award-winning group.

ANGELO STATE UNIVERSITY'S MASCOT is a big sheep or ram. Students call themselves the Ram Family and say they are "Loud and Ram Fam Proud!"

Fort Concho
(El Fuerte Concho)

F is for Fort Concho, the old frontier army post that is now a museum.

When Fort Concho started in 1867, a soldier could get three hot meals every day, a cot to sleep on, and $13 per month. Many young men left their homes to go to West Texas and protect the frontier. Fort Concho had at least 40 stone buildings spread out over more than 1,600 acres with a staff of 400–500 soldiers, officers, and supporting workers.

In 1889, the last soldiers marched away from Fort Concho, and the empty stone buildings soon began to fall apart. Almost 40 years later, volunteers helped rebuild and save the fort. It became a National Historic Landmark in 1961.

Some of the soldiers were African American men who joined when the Civil War ended. The Native Americans of the Great Plains had not seen black troops before, so they gave them the nickname "Buffalo Soldiers," equating their curly, dark hair style and courage to that of their sacred buffalo. 23 Buffalo Soldiers received the Medal of Honor for helping tame the frontier.

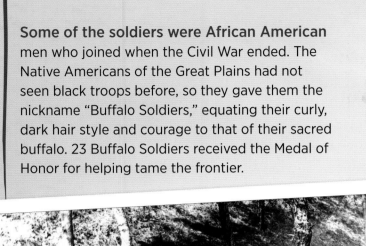

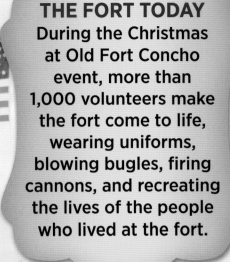

THE FORT TODAY

During the Christmas at Old Fort Concho event, more than 1,000 volunteers make the fort come to life, wearing uniforms, blowing bugles, firing cannons, and recreating the lives of the people who lived at the fort.

Goodfellow Air Force Base
(La Base Aérea de Goodfellow)

G is for Goodfellow Air Force Base. People who live on Goodfellow Air Force Base practice military skills that help protect America.

Though the U.S. Air Force is known for its airplanes and pilots, there is no flight training on this base. People come to Goodfellow from all over the United States to study three special kinds of military skills:

- Intelligence: training in languages, critical thinking, problem solving, and planning
- Cryptology: training in computer science, coding, and new ways to protect secret messages
- Military firefighting: training to put out fires on planes, trucks, and buildings, which is important for working on planes, around the base, or wherever in the world military people might be stationed

The men and women in the U.S. Air Force, Army, Navy, Coast Guard, and Marine Corps volunteer throughout San Angelo. A special activity they host is STARBASE Goodfellow, where kids can take STEM classes. Activities include robotics, rocketry, computer-aided design, and circuits.

One Big Flag
Every year a special group from Goodfellow holds a huge American flag on Centennial Bridge on Independence Day.

Heritage Park
(La Parque del Patrimonio)

H is for Heritage Park, a small park that shows how important ranching is to San Angelo.

When you scan the QR codes on the information displays in Heritage Park, you can watch videos about the ranchers who settled West Texas. One is a tribute to Henry Pfluger, who was born in Germany and started a farm on land called Brushy Knob. Lots of his grandchildren live in San Angelo and can trace their family tree back to the first Pfluger farmers.

DEFINITION:
Pocket Park (noun): a small, open space carved out of the middle of a city. It is a quiet place that is just big enough to welcome visitors while still being small enough to feel like a special get-away spot.

Heritage Park is located in the middle of San Angelo where ranchers used to feed their herds and ride their horses. The park has a rainwater capture system that shows how ranchers save water.

Heritage Park is a good place to sit and read beside the sculpture of Hank the Cowdog, the happiest detective on the ranch. This statue honors rancher John R. Erickson who wrote more than 63 books about Hank and his West Texas adventures.

International Waterlily Collection
(La Colección Internacional de Nenúfares)

I is for the International Waterlily Collection. There are seven ponds with more than 450 kinds of lilies, and more photos are taken here than anywhere else in San Angelo.

People come from all over the world to see the rare flowers at the International Waterlily Collection—lilies like the Blue Cloud from Australia and Texas Dawn, the official water lily of Texas.

The flowers of lilies are only a small part of the plant. Thick, long stems are buried in the mud under the water. Sometimes leaves surround the flowers, but often, they are underwater too. The flower of a lily lives for only three days or three nights, depending on whether the lily blooms in the day or night.

Ken Landon, who created the garden, is called the Indiana Jones of water lilies because he has been all over the world and braved snakes, alligators, and other creatures to collect very old or almost extinct water lilies. One of his most challenging trips was to the jungles of Mexico to search for a rare white star lily. Because he found it, he is able to create star lilies in many other colors.

WHEN CAN I SEE THE FLOWERS? The Waterlily Collection blooms from April through October, but the best time to see the flowers is September.

Jumano Tribe
(La Tribu Jumano)

J is for Jumano (say who-mah-no), the people who lived in West Texas and New Mexico long before Europeans migrated here.

In 2018, the Jumano and members of the Catholic Church in San Angelo worked together to have statues made of the Lady in Blue, a Jumano chief, and a child. The statues were created by sculptor Vic Payne, and you can see them on the banks of the Concho River.

This peaceful tribe farmed in one place, but when the growing season was over, they traveled from one side of the plains to the other, carrying food and tools to trade.

San Angelo in the movies: *The Needle and the Thread* is a documentary about the Jumano and the Lady in Blue. In 2019, the film was taken to the Vatican to be seen by Pope Francis.

A special part of Jumano history is their story about a lady in blue who visited them in the 1600s and told them about Jesus. At the same time, a nun in Spain named Marie de Ágreda said she talked with the Jumano, even though she never left her country and the Jumano never went to Spain. The members of the tribe believed in the teachings of the Lady in Blue and thousands of them became Christians.

Kids Kingdom
(El Reino de los Niños)

K is for Kids Kingdom, a park in downtown San Angelo that was designed by children.

The San Angelo parks staff and a design company met with 20–30 children and let the kids design anything they wanted. That's why this park has a rocket ship, a boat, slides, tubes, bridges, tunnels made out of huge tires, rope swings, and climbing ropes. The kids thought of it all, and the city worked with volunteers to build it.

When the final design was ready, more than 2,000 volunteers worked together to build Kids Kingdom in just seven days. Since it is on the River Walk, children in San Angelo can run, jump, and swing through the park on any day of the week.

A COOL VIEW

If you stand on the deck at the Visitors Center and look across the Concho River, the Kids Kingdom looks like an old frontier city with kids leaping and jumping through their own version of San Angelo.

Libraries (Las Bibliotecas)

L is for libraries. San Angelo has four libraries where you can read and borrow all kinds of books for free.

The children's library has books, special reading seats, costumes, and story time. The STEAM Central Makerspace has almost 200 STEAM programs and tools like a 3D printer, a laser cutter, and a die cutting machine.

The biggest library in San Angelo is the Stephens Central Branch Library. It has four floors and looks like a giant ship with windows that look like waves. Inside, the library is colorful and fun. There's even a little café where you can buy a snack. On the top floor, you can go outside to read a book or watch parades on the streets below.

Two for you and two for me and two for you: There are 250,000 books in the San Angelo libraries. That is so many books that every person in town could check out two books and there would still be books left over.

Monarch butterfly
(La Mariposa Monarca)

M is for the monarch butterfly. Thousands of monarchs visit San Angelo as they fly south for the winter and north for the summer.

The monarch butterflies make this trip every year, and they are the only kind of butterfly that migrates two ways like birds do. We still don't know how monarchs know where to go, but scientists think it could be the magnetic pull of the earth and the position of the sun.

Monarch butterflies bunch together to stay warm. Tens of thousands of monarchs can group together on a single tree. One butterfly weighs less than one gram—less than a raisin or a stick of gum—but thousands of butterflies in a group can weigh a lot. Sometimes, they can even break tree branches.

ON THE FLY

Monarchs can travel between 50–100 miles a day. It can take up to two months to complete their journey. The farthest a monarch has ever traveled was 265 miles in one day, which is almost the distance from San Angelo to Dallas.

Nature Center
(El Centro de la Naturaleza)

N is for Nature Center. This is a safe place for animals that can't live in the wild in West Texas. The Nature Center adopts wild animals that have been injured and special kinds of pets that owners can't keep.

The San Angelo Nature Center has animals that are native to the Southwest region of the United States. The staff and volunteers show visitors how to take care of the animals and teach important things like the differences between poisonous and nonpoisonous snakes. You can also see fossils, minerals, and rocks at the Nature Center.

Roger, the blue and yellow macaw, is one of the Nature Center's most popular animals because he has beautiful, colorful feathers and can talk!

Some people believe **chameleons change color** based on their surroundings, but that isn't true. Chameleons change color because of their moods. For example, when Karma, the veiled chameleon, is upset or scared, she turns a dark blue and purple color.

DID YOU KNOW?
Green iguanas like Balthazar are typically found in Central and South America. Iguanas can grow to be five feet from head to tail. Balthazar loves grapes, hot afternoons, and sleeping in the sun. While green iguanas are beautiful, they can be mean, so don't pet them in the wild.

Oscar Ruffini, Architect
(El Arquitecto)

O is for Oscar Ruffini, San Angelo's first architect. Architects draw designs and write instructions for buildings to be built.

Oscar always wore a black suit, a black tie, and a black hat. He ate the same meals every day at the same time and in the same place. For breakfast, he ate bacon and eggs at the City Café, and every afternoon, he ate a scoop of vanilla ice cream with a cherry on top at the Concho Drug Store.

Methodist   Catholic   Baptist
THREE OF SAN ANGELO'S CHURCHES

Oscar designed most of the first churches in town and 36 buildings in downtown San Angelo. You can see his work wherever San Angelo's oldest buildings still stand.

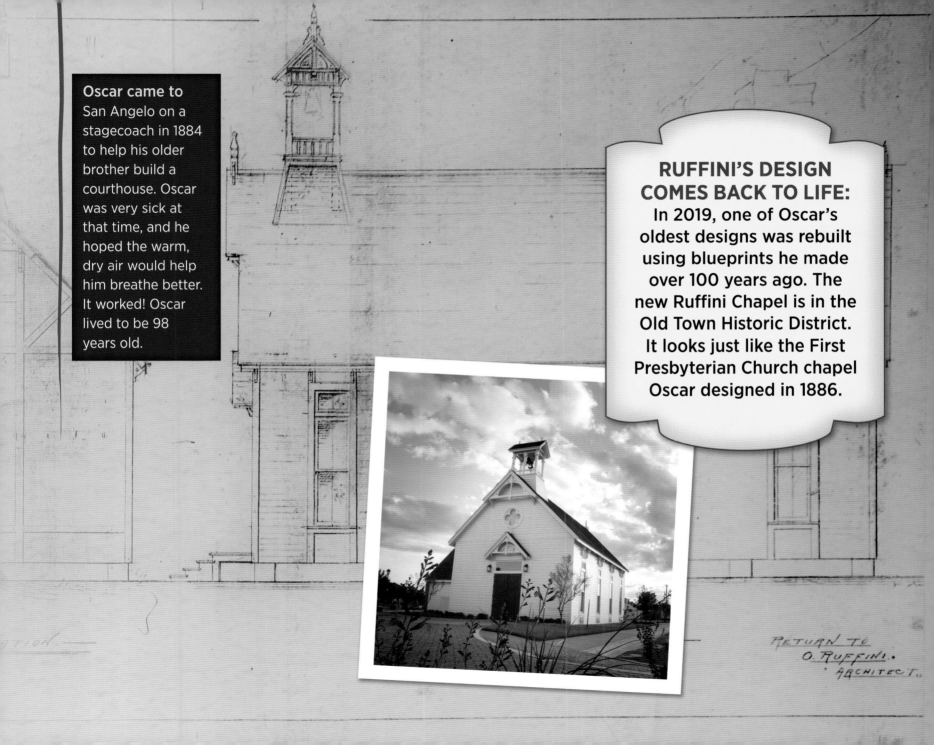

Oscar came to San Angelo on a stagecoach in 1884 to help his older brother build a courthouse. Oscar was very sick at that time, and he hoped the warm, dry air would help him breathe better. It worked! Oscar lived to be 98 years old.

RUFFINI'S DESIGN COMES BACK TO LIFE: In 2019, one of Oscar's oldest designs was rebuilt using blueprints he made over 100 years ago. The new Ruffini Chapel is in the Old Town Historic District. It looks just like the First Presbyterian Church chapel Oscar designed in 1886.

RETURN TO
O. RUFFINI.
ARCHITECT.

Performing Arts Center
(El Cento de las artes Escénicas)

P is for the Performing Arts Center, also known as the PAC, where you can watch dance, theater, and music shows.

There are lots of ways to join San Angelo's performance fun. San Angelo Broadway Academy performs musicals, and the San Angelo Symphony puts on musical concerts. Every Christmas season, dancers perform the *Nutcracker*, bringing flowers, candy canes, mice, and toy soldiers to life.

Another part of the PAC is across the street from the big building. The Stephens Performing Arts Center has two smaller performance stages and big practice rooms for ballet and theater classes.

BOX O' FUN
One of the theatres in the PAC is called a Black Box. It's a room with plain black walls and a flat floor. The local group Be Theatre uses this space in many new ways, like letting the audience throw popcorn at the actors during a funny summer show called a melodrama.

In 2017, San Angelo took an old auditorium and turned it into a performing arts center. The Murphey Performance Hall is so big that visiting shows can set up giant scenery and props on stage.

Quilts (Los Edredones)

Q is for Quilts. These special covers do more than just keep you warm.

Many years ago in San Angelo, women went to events called quilting bees to help each other sew quilts. They gathered to sew, talk, laugh, and share their quilt patterns. At a quilting bee, women would work together to sew several quilts at the same time. Together, they could finish many quilts in a single day instead of a quilt taking weeks or months to finish alone.

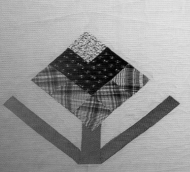

Not all stories are told in books. Some quilts tell the story of a family's life. A patchwork quilt might be made of pieces of fabric from Dad's shirts and Sister's dresses, and just seeing it brings back memories of that time. Each design, stitch, and piece of fabric in a quilt tells a story of the person who made it.

THE BUZZ ABOUT A QUILTING BEE

Quilting is still an important part of life in San Angelo. There are groups that sew quilts for veterans, babies, and people in hospitals. But quilters from long ago would be shocked to see the big, robotic quilting machines that create patterns based on signals from a computer. In the Stephens Downtown Branch of the library, 264 quilts were made last year using the modern sewing and cutting equipment.

Rodeo (El Rodeo)

R is for rodeo. There are bulls that don't want to be ridden, horses that try to toss off their riders, and riders who can make their horses turn very quickly in small spaces.

The San Angelo Rodeo Parade happens on the first Saturday of the stock show and rodeo as the start of the event. This parade is one of the largest parades held in San Angelo each year and is a town favorite.

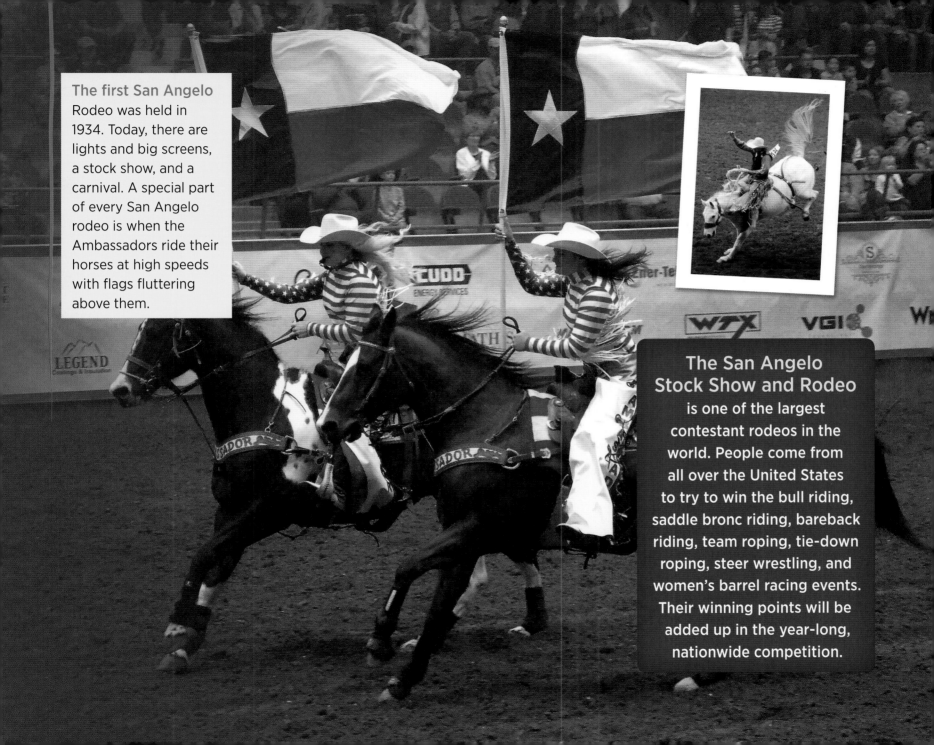

The first San Angelo Rodeo was held in 1934. Today, there are lights and big screens, a stock show, and a carnival. A special part of every San Angelo rodeo is when the Ambassadors ride their horses at high speeds with flags fluttering above them.

The San Angelo Stock Show and Rodeo is one of the largest contestant rodeos in the world. People come from all over the United States to try to win the bull riding, saddle bronc riding, bareback riding, team roping, tie-down roping, steer wrestling, and women's barrel racing events. Their winning points will be added up in the year-long, nationwide competition.

Sheep (La oveja)

S is for sheep. There are painted sheep all over San Angelo, and these colorful, creative sheep have become a symbol of San Angelo.

In the 1800s, West Texas was a great place to raise sheep. One shepherd could travel with 1,500 sheep. With all of these sheep around, San Angelo was called "the wool center of the world."

The city of San Angelo started the tradition of painted sheep in 2007 when they stopped having a Miss Wool pageant. Local artists paint different designs on the sculptures so that no two sheep look alike. Today, there are 101 painted sheep all around the city.

Where there is a painted sheep, there is a pun. Look at these sheeptacular names: Ed-ewe-cate, When Ewe Are Hungry, EWE-nique, Happy Trails to EWE, Don't Ewe Mess with Texas, and 94 more names, all just as punny.

Trains (Los Trenes)

Tis for Trains. The train coming through San Angelo was very important in the early days.

San Angelo owes much of its early history to trains. People worked hard to build a bridge over the Concho River so that trains wouldn't pass San Angelo. In 1888, the Santa Fe Railway came to San Angelo bringing supplies, livestock, and oil. Today, there are still about 26 Texas Pacifico trains that run through the middle of San Angelo each month.

DID YOU KNOW?
A yardmaster is a person who schedules the trains coming in and going out of town. Unit trains all carry the same thing and go to the same place. Manifest trains carry many different cargos and go different places. The yard master knows where each train goes and what it carries.

The Orient-Santa Fe Depot is now the railway museum. At the museum, you can see all the bells and whistles from the railrailroad—even a real train engine.

Uniform (El uniforme)

U is for Uniform, a type of clothing worn by members of a team or group. Uniform means things have the same form, color, or style.

In San Angelo, many people wear uniforms. You can find police officers, firefighters, members of the military, and healthcare workers in our city by the uniforms they wear. Sometimes they wear a patch with the name of their group on it. They may wear special badges on their uniform that show honors they have won.

WHAT ABOUT YOU?
Do you have a uniform? Do you wear something special for school or sports? Even a T-shirt can be a uniform, if everyone in your group is wearing it.

The Fort Worth Police Pipes and Drums visits San Angelo wearing their Scottish kilt uniform. They play bagpipes and drums for special events.

Firefighters wear protective jackets and helmets when they fight a fire. They have on heavy gloves and boots that won't catch on fire, and they carry oxygen tanks on their backs.

Vistas
(Las Vistas Panorámicas)

V is for Vistas, which are views that let you see a long, long way.

Vista is the word used to describe the kind of view you might see from a mountaintop. It means you can see for a long distance without buildings or trees in your way. One of the exciting things about San Angelo is that the beautiful vistas look different at sunrise, daytime, or sunset.

Stand on a bridge downtown or go to the observation deck of the San Angelo Museum of Fine Arts. You will see the vista of San Angelo spread out before you.

Ask an adult to drive you around the shore of Lake Nasworthy until you find a spot with nothing in your way and you can look across the water.

For a vista view: Go to the top of Hillside Drive and look toward Twin Buttes.

Get up early and watch the sunrise or find a spot after supper to sit and watch the sunset.

Wings (Las Alas)

W is for wings. Planes, helicopters, drones, birds, and sometimes even people fly over San Angelo with all kinds of wings.

The San Angelo Regional Airport, also called Mathis Field, serves more than 66,000 passengers and flies almost 85,000 air operations each year. There are also more than 150 aircrafts based at Mathis Field.

At Mathis Field, you can see pilots fly the T-38 Talon and practice what is called a "touch-and-go" landing, where the plane touches the ground for a second and then takes off again. Goodfellow Air Force Base was a pilot training command during WWII, so there is a long history of pilots practicing flying in San Angelo.

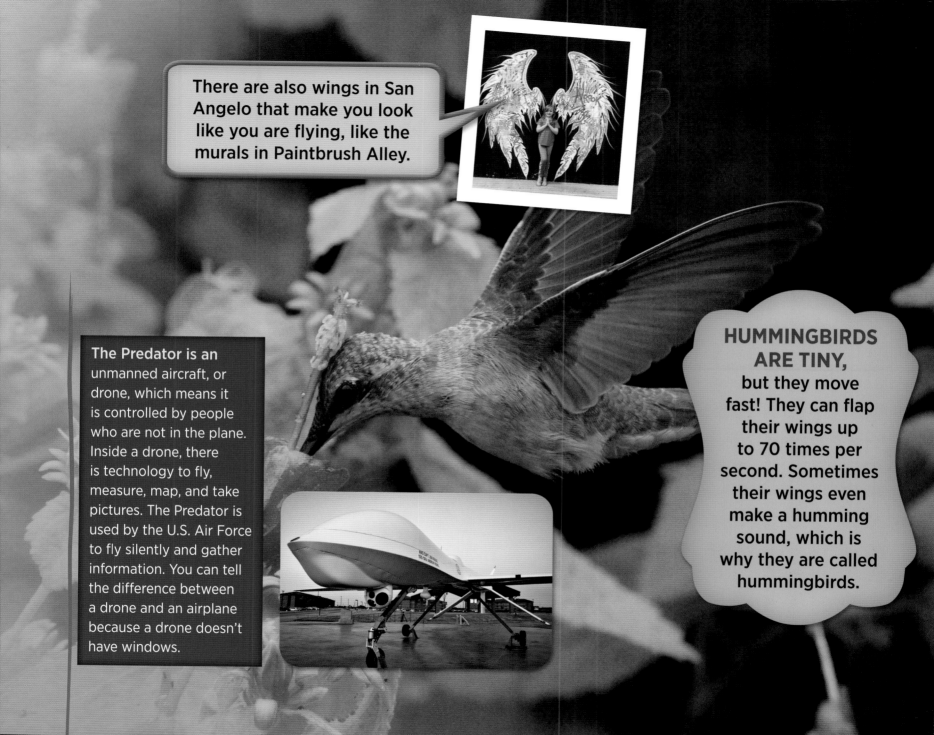

There are also wings in San Angelo that make you look like you are flying, like the murals in Paintbrush Alley.

The Predator is an unmanned aircraft, or drone, which means it is controlled by people who are not in the plane. Inside a drone, there is technology to fly, measure, map, and take pictures. The Predator is used by the U.S. Air Force to fly silently and gather information. You can tell the difference between a drone and an airplane because a drone doesn't have windows.

HUMMINGBIRDS ARE TINY, but they move fast! They can flap their wings up to 70 times per second. Sometimes their wings even make a humming sound, which is why they are called hummingbirds.

X Marks the Spot
(La X Marca el Lugar)

The treasure of San Angelo is the Concho Pearl. This treasure is so rare that it has been hunted for hundreds of years, and that is why San Angelo is known as the Pearl of West Texas.

Over 400 years ago, the tribes who lived in West Texas found that the freshwater mussels in the Concho River had pink and purple pearls inside. In 1654, the governor of New Mexico sent soldiers on a long, long trip to West Texas to search for *Tesoro de San Angelo*, the treasured pearls of San Angelo. The troops found the mussel shells and named the river the Concho, which means "shell" in Spanish. Some people say the rare Concho pearls they found may be in the Spanish crown jewels.

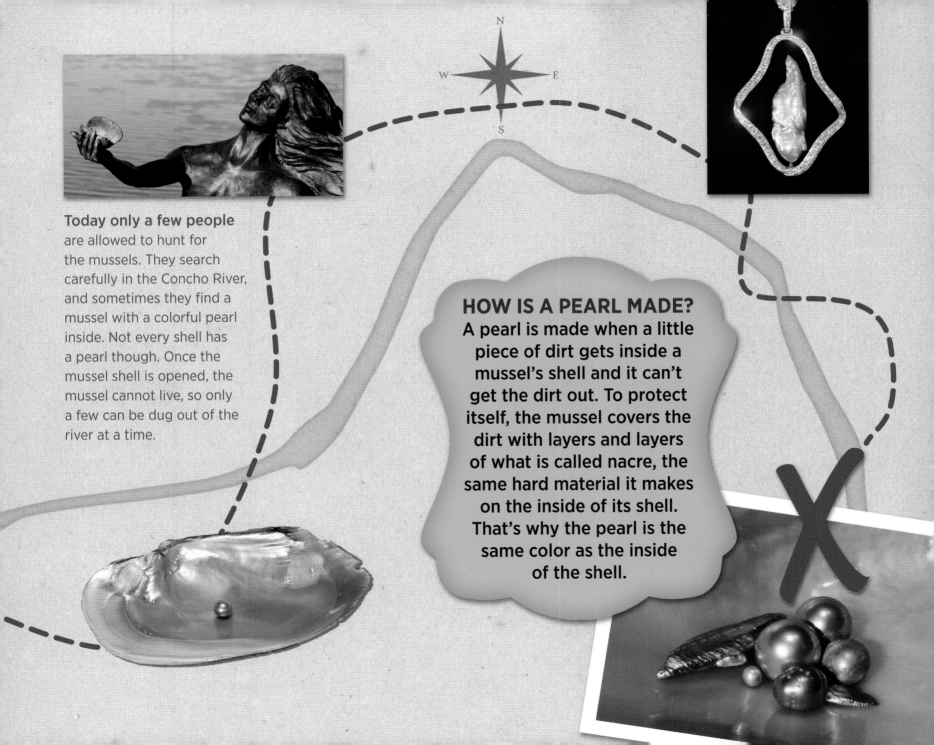

Today only a few people are allowed to hunt for the mussels. They search carefully in the Concho River, and sometimes they find a mussel with a colorful pearl inside. Not every shell has a pearl though. Once the mussel shell is opened, the mussel cannot live, so only a few can be dug out of the river at a time.

HOW IS A PEARL MADE?
A pearl is made when a little piece of dirt gets inside a mussel's shell and it can't get the dirt out. To protect itself, the mussel covers the dirt with layers and layers of what is called nacre, the same hard material it makes on the inside of its shell. That's why the pearl is the same color as the inside of the shell.

Yellow Fields and Flowers
(Los Campos y Las Flores Amarillos)

Y is for yellow fields and flowers that cover San Angelo with a glow like sunshine. Texas is known for bluebonnets, but many fields in San Angelo are covered with bright yellow flowers in the springtime.

Coreopsis:
One of the happiest flowers in San Angelo is coreopsis. This flower stands for cheerfulness, hope, and devotion. It is often given to cheer up people who are sad or who are in the hospital.

Wild Mustard Flowers:
The brightest of all yellow fields is covered in Wild Mustard flowers. Some mustard plants can be ground up and used as a spice for food.

Greenthread: Fields of Greenthread can be used to make Navaho or Hopi tea if boiled in hot water. It tastes like green tea and was used as medicine.

Wild Yellow Lily: You are probably not surprised that wild yellow lilies love sunshine. They grow beside roads and along streams or rivers. They smell so good that hummingbirds, butterflies, and bees love them.

Cactus: Even the prickly pear cactus adds to San Angelo's color. Their yellow flowers bring bees right out of their honeycombs.

Zapatos (shoes)

Z is for Los Zapatos, which means shoes in English. San Angelo has two shops downtown that have been making footwear since San Angelo was barely a town.

The *zapatos* that are original to San Angelo are custom-made *botas*—or boots. M. L. Leddy and J. L. Mercer make boots completely by hand that are specially designed for each customer. In the boot stores, there are sewing machines, sanders, sole stitchers, and other machines that have been used for over 100 years. Flowers, stars, initials, and fancy designs make each boot special for the owner.

Every boot owner has a page in M. L. Leddy's record books. Foot sizes of more than 250,000 customers have been carefully drawn by hand. Boots of presidents, royalty, rock stars, and cowboys have a hand-written code inside each boot top that allows Leddy's to trace each pair to its original owner. The skilled workers at the shop each have a specialty—they do one thing—like building a boot heel.

LAST, BUT NOT LEAST:
These zapatos are made using a foot-shaped mold called a "last," making sure the finished boot fits just right. Each person who orders a custom boot has two lasts made to match his or her feet. These zapatos really are made to last.

San Angelo History Timeline

Early San Angelo—Many Native American tribes lived in the Concho Valley and their trails crossed present day San Angelo. Bison and deer roamed the land.

1500—Spanish explorers claimed the area we now call Texas.

1600s—The Jumano Tribe and the Lady in Blue shared a common story.

1654—The governor of New Mexico sent troops to the Concho Valley to search for the treasure of San Angelo.

1821—Mexico achieved its independence from Spain and the Concho Valley became part of Mexico.

1836—The Republic of Texas controlled the area.

1845—Texas became a state.

1858—The Butterfield Overland Stage included San Angelo on its stagecoach route.

1861–65—The Concho Valley became part of the Confederate States of America.

1866—The Goodnight-Loving Trail came through San Angelo to drive cattle to western markets, following the Concho River for a considerable distance.

1867—Fort Concho was built along the banks of the Concho River to protect frontier settlements, and to patrol and map the vast West Texas region.

1870—Bart DeWitt bought 320 acres of land to develop a town, named Santa Angela for his late wife Carolina Angela de la Garza.

1870–90—Sheep raising boomed, eventually numbering over a million sheep.

1876—The first subscription school was built.

1882—San Angelo became county seat of Tom Green County.

1884—Architect Oscar Ruffini arrived; the first public school opened; *San Angelo Standard Newspaper* was established.

1888—Santa Fe Railroad came to town.

1889—The last federal troops left San Angelo after one last salute was fired and the Fort Concho flag was lowered.

1900—San Angelo was the largest range-cattle shipping station in the United States.

1903—San Angelo Independent School District started.

1905—Kansas City, Mexico, and Orient Railway came to San Angelo.

1923—Santa Rita oil blew in, starting the oil boom in West Texas; M. L. Leddy and J. L. Mercer opened boot making shops downtown.

1928—The Orient Railway was sold to Santa Fe Railway; San Angelo State University started.

1929—The Cactus Hotel and the City Auditorium were built.

1931—JM and Margaret Shannon Foundation was established for hospitals.

1934—The first San Angelo Rodeo took place.

1940—Goodfellow Air Force Base was constructed as a temporary base.

1947—San Angelo College's administration building was completed.

1951—The first Miss Wool of Texas Pageant was held.

1956—Goodfellow AFB became a permanent installation; San Angelo Stadium was built on Knickerbocker.

1957—President Dwight Eisenhower visited to inspect drought damage.

1958—Miss Wool became a national pageant; Central High School was built for $3.5 million, designed for 2,150 students.

1959—San Angelo Coliseum was built for San Angelo Stock Show and Rodeo.

1969—San Angelo College became Angelo State University.

1970—Municipal Airport was built at Mathis Field.

1974—Chicken Farm Art Center was started.

1980—Howard College began offering classes in San Angelo.

1985—San Angelo Museum of Fine Arts opened in Fort Concho.

1989—San Angelo opened the Nature Center to the public beside Lake Nasworthy.

1993—A RUDAT study started linking the downtown area to new construction over the river.

2000—San Angelo Museum of Fine Arts moved into its new building.

2005—The International Water Lily Collection got a home in the Civic League Park.

2006—Kids Kingdom opened.

2007—San Angelo's painted sheep project began.

2011—Tom Green County Library moved into a remodeled Hemphill-Wells department store location.

2017—Brenda Gunter was elected the first female mayor of San Angelo; the old City Auditorium was transformed into the Performing Arts Center.

2018—Work on Heritage Park started; the Lady in Blue statue was dedicated.

2019—Mark Meyers was named one of CNN's Top 10 Heroes for his Peaceful Valley Donkey Rescue; the Pop Art Museum started in an old bowling alley.